The Story of
JESUS

written by Dandi

For years the world waited, expecting the coming of a Savior. Then a young girl named Mary received a surprise visit from an angel. "God has chosen *you*, Mary," said the angel, "to be the mother of His only son!"

So Mary and Joseph were married. About this time, an order went out demanding that all the Jews travel to their families' hometowns to pay taxes. Mary and Joseph would have to go to Bethlehem. Mary was close to her time to give birth. This long journey was not what she and Joseph expected.

The journey to Bethlehem was long and rough.

"It will be okay, Mary," Joseph told her as they entered Bethlehem. "I will find a room for you at an inn. You'll have a nice, comfortable place to have the baby."

But Bethlehem was crowded. Every inn Joseph tried turned him down. "No room here!" they said.

Joseph grew anxious for Mary. This was not what he had expected when he brought his wife to Bethlehem.

The last innkeeper told Joseph his inn was full too. But when he saw Mary, he said, "Well, I guess you could stay in the stable."

So in the stable, with the cows and donkeys, and roosters, Joseph made a place for Mary. "I know this is not what you expected," Joseph said.

But Mary smiled at her husband. She knew God would take care of them.

There in the stable, Mary gave birth to the baby Jesus. She wrapped the baby in strips of cloth and laid him in a manger. It was the most important night in the history of the world. Instead of a royal bed of golden cushions, the Savior lay in a bed of straw – not what might be expected for the King of kings.

Out in the countryside, a young shepherd boy expected nothing more than to pass the night as he always did, guarding the sheep from wolves. Poor and unimportant in the world, the shepherd boy never expected to be part of the miraculous night that first Christmas.

Suddenly a light shone in the heavens! The frightened little shepherd boy ran to the other shepherds.

"Don't be afraid," said an angel. "I am bringing you the best news ever! The Savior you have waited for has been born tonight in a manger in Bethlehem!" Then a host of angels joined, singing, "Glory to God in the highest, and peace on earth to all who please God!"

"We must go find the Newborn King!" said the little shepherd boy. And he trembled with expectation!

The shepherds ran through the countryside and into the village. They shouted the good news to everyone they met. "The Savior is born!"

The little shepherd boy led the way to the stable in Bethlehem. When they saw the baby Jesus, they knew. Everything was exactly as they had been told by the angels. This truly was the son of God!

Far, far away wise men began their journey. Kings themselves, they had received a special message that the King of all kings had been born. They didn't know what to expect. They only knew that they had to see this King for themselves. The wise men collected their gifts of gold, frankincense, and myrrh. Then they mounted camels and followed the brightest star in the heavens.

The wise men and the shepherds came to see the Christ Child and found much more than they expected:

'I never could have guessed that God would include me in His great plan for the world,' thought the shepherd boy.

'This Baby is greater than any king, greater than we expected,' thought the wise men.

'Such a marvelous plan!' thought Joseph. 'Only our great God would send His one son to earth as a baby to guide us!'

'I never expected to be so blessed,' thought Mary.

People today are still finding the Christ Child and discovering for themselves that Jesus is much, much more than they could have expected.